ISRAEL
AND THE
ARAB TURMOIL

[For a list of books published under the auspices of the
WORKING GROUP ON ISLAMISM AND THE INTERNATIONAL ORDER,
please see page 57.]

HERBERT & JANE DWIGHT WORKING GROUP ON ISLAMISM AND THE INTERNATIONAL ORDER

ESSAY SERIES: THE GREAT UNRAVELING: THE REMAKING OF THE MIDDLE EAST

ISRAEL
AND THE
ARAB TURMOIL

Itamar Rabinovich

HOOVER INSTITUTION PRESS
Stanford University   Stanford, California

The Hoover Institution on War, Revolution and Peace, founded at Stanford University in 1919 by Herbert Hoover, who went on to become the thirty-first president of the United States, is an interdisciplinary research center for advanced study on domestic and international affairs. The views expressed in its publications are entirely those of the authors and do not necessarily reflect the views of the staff, officers, or Board of Overseers of the Hoover Institution.

www.hoover.org

Hoover Institution Press Publication No. 647

Hoover Institution at Leland Stanford Junior University, Stanford, California, 94305-6010

First printing 2014
21 20 19 18 17 16 15 14   9 8 7 6 5 4 3 2 1

Manufactured in the United States of America

The paper used in this publication meets the minimum requirements of the American National Standard for Information Sciences— Permanence of Paper for Printed Library Materials, ANSI/NISO Z39.48-1992. ⊗

Cataloging-in-Publication Data is available from the Library of Congress.
ISBN 978-0-8179-1735-7 (pbk.: alk. paper)
ISBN 978-0-8179-1736-4 (epub)
ISBN 978-0-8179-1737-1 (mobi)
ISBN 978-0-8179-1738-8 (PDF)

*The Hoover Institution gratefully acknowledges
the following individuals and foundations
for their significant support of the*

HERBERT AND JANE DWIGHT WORKING GROUP
ON ISLAMISM AND THE INTERNATIONAL ORDER:

Herbert and Jane Dwight

Beall Family Foundation

Stephen Bechtel Foundation

Lynde and Harry Bradley Foundation

Mr. and Mrs. Clayton W. Frye Jr.

Lakeside Foundation

CONTENTS

SERIES FOREWORD

The Great Unraveling:
The Remaking of the Middle East

IT'S A MANTRA, but it is also true: the Middle East is being unmade and remade. The autocracies that gave so many of these states the appearance of stability are gone, their dreaded rulers dispatched to prison or exile or cut down by young people who had yearned for the end of the despotisms. These autocracies were large prisons, and in 2011, a storm overtook that stagnant world. The spectacle wasn't pretty, but prison riots never are. In the Fertile Crescent, the work of the colonial cartographers—Gertrude Bell, Winston Churchill, and Georges Clemenceau—are in play as they have never been before. Arab nationalists were given to lamenting that they lived in nation-states "invented" by Western powers in the aftermath of the Great War. Now, a century later, with the ground burning in Lebanon, Syria, and Iraq and the religious sects at war, not even the most ardent nationalists can be sure that they can put in place anything better than the old order.

Men get used to the troubles they know, and the Greater Middle East seems fated for grief and breakdown. Outside powers approach it with dread; merciless political contenders have the run of it. There is swagger in Iran and a belief that the radical theocracy can bully its rivals into submission. There was a period when the United States provided a modicum of order in these Middle Eastern lands. But pleading fatigue, and financial scarcity at home, we have all but announced the end of that stewardship. We are poorer for that abdication, and the Middle East is thus left to the mercy of predators of every kind.

We asked a number of authors to give this spectacle of disorder their best try. We imposed no rules on them, as we were sure their essays would take us close to the sources of the malady.

FOUAD AJAMI
Senior Fellow, Hoover Institution—
Cochairman, Herbert and Jane Dwight Working Group
on Islamism and the International Order

CHARLES HILL
Distinguished Fellow of the Brady-Johnson Program
in Grand Strategy at Yale University;
Research Fellow, Hoover Institution—
Cochairman, Herbert and Jane Dwight Working Group
on Islamism and the International Order

Israel and the Arab Turmoil

ITAMAR RABINOVICH

ISRAEL LOOKS AT THE ARAB TURMOIL through a fractured lens: that of a powerful but anxious state, an important actor in Middle Eastern politics not fully integrated in the region, at peace with some Arab states and in conflict with other parts of the Arab and Muslim world.

During several decades, Israel's leadership, like its predecessors in prestate Israel, saw the Arab world in terms of a "zero-sum game." By the late 1930s, it transpired that a military conflict with the Palestinian Arabs was inevitable if a Jewish state was to be established and the Arab states adopted the Palestinian cause as their own and took charge of it. Within a few years, the Arab-Jewish conflict in and over Palestine was transformed by the 1948 war into the Arab-Israel conflict. The failure to end that war with a peace settlement led to the festering of the conflict and to three additional major wars—1956, 1967, and 1973.

From this perspective, success and empowerment of the Arab collective was seen as detrimental to Israel. Israel despaired of breaking Arab hostility and therefore focused on seeking the cracks in that wall—minorities, rivalries—or on circumventing it by building bridges to the region's "periphery"—Turkey, Iran, and Ethiopia—non-Arab states equally concerned with the power of pan-Arab nationalism in its heyday in the 1950s and 1960s.

This perspective began to change in 1979 with the signing of the Egyptian-Israeli peace treaty. Having made peace with the most important Arab state, did it make sense for Israel to continue to look for cracks in the wall of hostility or circumvent it, or did it make more sense to expand the opening and seek a comprehensive change in, if not a full transformation of, its relationship with the Arab world?

In the event, progress along such lines was slow and problematic. The peace process was suspended in practice for more than a decade. The Egyptian-Israeli peace treaty survived adversity, but its scope was limited to a bare minimum. First Anwar Sadat and then Hosni Mubarak followed a policy of a "cold peace" with Israel, keeping the essentials of the agreement but restricting the development of normal relations. This reality did not in fact bother the Israeli leadership that had its own ambivalent view of full peace and integration in the region. In any event, failure to move forward in resolving the Israeli-Palestinian conflict, the ongoing conflict with Syria, Iraq's emergence as a major Arab power, and the regional ramifications of the Iranian revolution perpetuated the state of conflict and blunted the impact of Israeli-Egyptian peace.

The renewal of the peace process under the auspices of the Bush administration in Madrid in 1991 exposed the complexity of the effort to normalize Israeli's relationship with its Arab environment. In 1993, Israel signed the Oslo

Accord with the PLO, and Israel and the Palestinian national movement went through the act of mutual recognition and charted a road map for a resolution of their conflict. In theory, this should have paved the way for accelerated normalization with Egypt and other Arab states. In practice, Israel's effort to use the agreement with the Palestinians in order to integrate itself into the region, most notably through Middle East economic conferences, provoked a negative Egyptian reaction. The Egyptian leadership (and in a different fashion, the Syrian one) was horrified by the vision Israel's foreign minister, Shimon Peres, put forth in his book *The New Middle East* and in his concept of peace with Syria in late 1995 and early 1996. Peres was the first Israeli leader to formulate a view of Israel's relationship with the Arab world departing from the "zero-sum" concept of earlier decades. But while Peres genuinely saw economic cooperation as a key to a stable peace in a more prosperous region, Egyptians, Syrians, and other Arabs saw it as neocolonialism, a sophisticated and cunning Israeli strategy to control the region. In the Syrian case, this remained a hypothetical issue, but the Egyptian political establishment, represented most notably by Foreign Minister Amr Moussa, while maintaining the peace treaty with Israel and offering some help in advancing the peace process, in fact saw Israel mostly as a competitor, threatening Egyptian primacy or hegemony. Egypt used the nuclear issue in order to undermine the multilateral track of the peace process. At home, Mubarak's regime allowed virulent criticism of Israel by Islamists and neo-Nasserite opposition groups as a way of building a common platform with the opposition on at least one issue.

The vision and threat of Israel at the end of a successful quest for a comprehensive peace settlement with its Arab neighbors becoming integrated into its environment evaporated in the late 1990s, when the momentum of the Madrid and Oslo processes was checked and the peace process came to a halt. Two major efforts were endorsed to renew a peace process and to complete Israel's negotiations with Syria and the Palestinians during the terms of Ehud Barak and Ehud Olmert, but both failed and the reality of Israel's relationship with its environment remained checkered: cold peace with Egypt and Jordan, partial normalization with several Arab states in North Africa and the Gulf, a continuation of Israel's conflict with a fragmented Palestinian counterpart, and continued conflict with Syria conducted mostly through Lebanon.

During the first decade of the current century, the Middle Eastern arena was transformed by the new roles played by Turkey and Iran. The twentieth century was exceptional in the region's history due to the absence of successor states of the Ottoman and Persian empires that had dominated the region for centuries. The Turkish state, shaped and inspired by Mustafa Kemal Ataturk, saw itself mostly as a European state with limited interest in the Middle East. Iran under the shah was preoccupied with the Soviet threat and domestic issues. It did play a role in the Middle East but not one commensurate with its potential. 1979 was to prove a year of great upheaval. The Islamic Revolution brought to power a regime seeking to export its design first and foremost to the Arab world, but the success of that policy was limited and its main achievements were the construction of a power base in

the Shiite community in Lebanon and an alliance with Syria. For both Turkey and Iran, 2003
was in that regard a turning point. In Turkey,
Recep Tayyip Erdogan came to power and began
to pursue a new foreign policy. Rebuffed by
Europe, Turkey under an Islamist government
was now seeking a hegemonic role in the Middle
East. The American invasion of Iraq and the
destruction of Saddam Hussein's regime removed
a significant barrier for Iran's ayatollahs. Iran
could now look for paramount influence in a
Shiite-dominated Iraq and accelerate its drive
for influence in other parts of the Middle East.
The regional politics of the Middle East were
not governed by a single issue, but the conflict
between Iran and its rivals was the single most
important variable in that system. This rivalry
served, among other things, to expose Israel's
problematic position in the region. It shared the
animosity toward the Iranian regime and the
opposition to its nuclear program and regional
ambitions with states like Egypt, Saudi Arabia,
and Jordan. But given the ongoing conflict with
the Palestinians, the limited scope of its peaceful relationship with Egypt and Jordan, and the

absence of a relationship with Saudi Arabia, it could not in fact become part of an effective anti-Iranian bloc.

THE OUTBREAK OF THE "ARAB SPRING"

Against this backdrop, Israel's reaction to the outbreak of what was initially named "the Arab Spring" and its early development in 2010 and 2011 was ambivalent. Israel's prime minister at the time, Benjamin Netanyahu, argued in a book he wrote in 1993 that the main obstacle to peace in the Middle East was the fact that all states in the region other than Israel were governed by non-democratic regimes. For real peace between Israel and its neighbors to be achieved, its neighbors had first to undergo a transition to democracy. In later years, the chief advocate of the need for democratic transformation in the Arab world in the ranks of the Israeli right wing was Natan Sharansky. But while Sharansky was unequivocal in his positive response to the events in Tunisia and Egypt, Netanyahu's response was ambivalent at best.

Most of Netanyahu's statements and responses in Israel were negative or doubtful. In his first public reaction to the Tunisian revolution on January 16, 2011, Netanyahu failed to refer to the democratic dimension of the event and chose to describe it as reflecting the unstable character of the Middle East. "The region we live in," Netanyahu said, "is unstable. We see that in several occasions in the geographic space within which we live." His initial response to the outburst of protest in Egypt on January 31, 2011, was similar—failure to mention the quest for democracy and stating his concern that events in Egypt could lead to the establishment of "a repressive regime of radical Islam." "In such a regime," said Netanyahu, "human rights are trampled and they constitute danger for peace." Nearly a year later, speaking at the opening of the Knesset session on October 31, 2011, Netanyahu spoke in some detail on developments in the Arab world and pinpointed his message: "If I had to summarize what we can expect in the region I would use two terms: instability and uncertainty. [. . .] To confront the uncertainty and instability facing us, we need two things:

power and responsibility." He further stated that "if religious extremism does not moderate its outlook, it is doubtful whether the great expectations that flowered with the flourishing of the Arab spring will materialize; it is possible that the implementation of these hopes will be postponed for the next generation."

A month later, Netanyahu offered a still darker perspective and added a note of criticism directed at those who saw the events in the Arab world in a positive optimistic light. "The Middle East is no place for the innocent," he said.

Last February I stood on this podium. Millions of Egyptian citizens filled the streets of Cairo. It was explained to me by commentators, and quite a few of my colleagues here at the opposition, that we are facing a new age of liberalism and progress that will wash away the old order. [. . .] I said that we are hoping that all of this will materialize but with all due respect for all hopes, it is most likely that an Islamist wave will wash the Arab states, an anti-Western, anti-liberal, anti-Israel and ultimately antidemocratic wave. I was told that I was trying to frighten the public but I do not see that we are on the wrong side of history, that I do not understand in what direction things are moving. They are moving but not forward towards progress. They are going backward. I chose to adapt our policy to reality and not to the heart's wishes. I am asking today who among us did not understand reality? Who among us misunderstood history?

Netanyahu and other Israeli politicians or analysts who emphasized the dark side of the Arab Spring from Israel's perspective were challenged by other voices—some of them more moderate politicians like Dan Meridor and Tzipi Livni and most forcefully by Peres, the president of the state of Israel. In April 1, 2011, Peres penned an op-ed in the *Guardian,* "We in Israel welcome the Arab Spring." Peres repeated his view on other occasions. In a speech in the Israeli parliament, the Knesset, on October 31, 2011, he stated that "undoubtedly, it is for the good of the whole region, including Israel, that a new order will arrive, that a Middle East will emerge with food to eat and freedom to breathe. The Struggle is unfolding and it cannot be judged by the first act or a single act."

On several occasions, speaking abroad or to international audiences, Netanyahu adopted a more positive tone with regard to events in the Arab world, but clearly his domestic statements reflected his true outlook. By choosing the term "the right side of history," Netanyahu was in fact taking issue with President Obama, who was initially supportive of what seemed to be an Arab Spring, seeking to place himself "on the right side of history." The first year of the Arab Spring was a period of sharp differences between the US president and the Israeli prime minister. The main bone of contention was Obama's quest for an Israeli-Palestinian settlement and his pressure on Netanyahu to go along with his policy.

We get a sense of the divergence between the Obama administration and the government of Netanyahu. In the memoirs of former Defense Secretary Robert Gates, *Duty: Memoirs of a Secretary at War* (2014), it's March 2011, Gates is on a visit to Israel, and he calls on Minister of Defense

Ehud Barak. Gates gives Barak his view of the events of the Arab Spring, reassures him that all is well with the Israel-Egypt treaty despite the turmoil in Egypt: "Speaking as a friend, I said now was the time for Israel not to hunker down but to act boldly in the region—to move on the peace process with the Palestinians, to reconcile with Turkey, and to help Jordan. I added that the good news about the turmoil in the region was that it was not about Israel or the United States— 'No one is burning U.S. or Israeli flags, yet'—but about internal problems in the Arab countries, and we needed to make sure that that remained the focus." Gates was to have a rougher time the next day when he drove up to Caesarea for a meeting with Prime Minister Netanyahu. He urged Netanyahu not to go into a "defensive crouch but to seize the moment with bold moves in the peace process. Bibi wasn't buying."

Differences of opinion regarding Iran's pursuit of a nuclear weapon were a second major bone of contention. These differences of opinion became related to the differing perspectives on the Arab Spring. Obama's initial policy in the Middle East sought to promote democratic change, to bring about an American reconciliation with the Arab and Muslim worlds, to resolve the Israeli-Palestinian conflict which he saw as a major reason for the tension between US and Arab and Muslim opinion, and to open a dialogue with Iran and Syria. This policy was reflected, among other things, in his 2009 Cairo speech, in the negative atmosphere that characterized Netanyahu's first visit to Washington shortly after Obama's inauguration and in the Obama administration's refusal to offer public support to the demonstrators against the Ayatollah's regime in 2009. In contrast, the Obama administration responded favorably to changes in Tunisia and Egypt, exerted pressure on Hosni Mubarak to leave office, and urged the Egyptian army to allow the free elections, which put Mohamed Morsi and the Muslim Brotherhood in power.

Netanyahu's variant response was shared by the Israeli right wing and quite a few Israeli centrists who were dubious of the prospect for a real transition to democracy in Egypt and other Arab countries, and concerned about the effect on Israel of instability and the rise of Islamist forces in neighboring countries and in the region at large. This Israeli caution was to some extent shaped by the 2006 elections in the Palestinian Authority. Prime Minister Ariel Sharon yielded to the pressure of President George W. Bush and allowed the elections, which brought Hamas to power in Gaza. Bush's outlook on democracy in the Arab world was different from that of Obama's, but in the eyes of many Israeli policy-makers and observers, the outcome was the same. As they saw it, every free election in an Arab or Muslim country was bound to end in an Islamist victory with negative implications for Israel. For Netanyahu and other right-wing Israeli politicians, this was not the time for Israel to take risks and to make territorial concessions, first and foremost in the Palestinian context, and expose Israel to unnecessary risks in an unstable environment.

Israeli concerns about the ramifications of what began as the Arab Spring in Tunisia and Egypt were twofold: a fear that the whole Arab world might be swept by a radical, mostly Islamist wave, and a more immediate and focused concern that the peace treaties with Egypt and Jordan would be undermined by a radical takeover in both countries. In the event, King Abdullah and the Hashemite regime in Jordan were able to weather the storm and survived the wave of opposition inspired by events in Tunisia and Egypt. In Egypt, developments from Israel's point of view were more complex, as described below.

There were two other elements in Israel's response to the first month of the Arab Spring. Netanyahu and his government looked at these events as related to the issue that preoccupied Netanyahu the most: Iran's quest for regional hegemony and a nuclear weapon. Mubarak's fall, in particular, as well as the threat to the conservative and moderate regimes in the region, was seen as an Iranian gain. Iran's opponents were weakened, and new opportunities became available to Tehran. And as can be seen in Netanyahu's statements quoted above, a separate debate was taking place over the relationship between the Arab Spring and the Palestinian issue. For Barack Obama and the Israel left, progress in the Israeli-Palestinian negotiations was more urgent than ever. Being "on the right side of history" meant that by putting an end to the Israeli-Palestinian conflict, Israel would make its own contribution to progress in the region and benefit from the transition to democracy. For Netanyahu and other spokesmen of the Israeli right wing, the changes in Egypt and elsewhere in the region meant that this was not the time to take risks or make territorial concessions.

Israel's calculus changed over time as the initial hopes for a far-reaching positive transformation in the Arab world were replaced by a more complex, often darker, reality: the domestic developments in Egypt, the Saudi suppression of the revolt in neighboring Bahrain, the outbreak of the Syrian civil war, and the civil war and Western intervention in Libya. By 2012, it became clear that the political status quo in the Arab world was not going to be altered to a democratic landscape anytime soon, that the initial wave of the Arab Spring had changed Arab politics, but that a long, complex process was unfolding and the current policy by Israel and others had to be nuanced. Furthermore, the underlying questions changed. As the Syrian civil war festered and the prospect loomed of Syria being broken up with far-reaching ramifications for the neighboring states of Iraq and Lebanon, Israeli leaders had to formulate a policy addressing instability and the danger of jihadi terrorism rather than with the prospect for democratic change. We will now examine Israel's thinking on these issues in several specific contexts.

EGYPT'S DOMESTIC CRISIS

For thirty years, Israel saw a cold peace with Egypt as a major pillar of its national security. Israel came to accept the very narrow scope of the peaceful relationship with Egypt. It realized that Mubarak's regime would not take on anti-Israeli and anti-Semitic manifestations in the Egyptian media and Egyptian public life, that he would be critical of several aspects of Israel's national security and regional policy (the nuclear issue, the Palestinian issue), and that he would not invest a genuine effort in putting an end to the smuggling of weapons into the Gaza Strip after the Hamas takeover in 2006. Other aspects of his policy—maintaining the essence of peace and nonbelligerency with Israel and common opposition to Iran—were deemed crucial.

Mubarak's fall from power raised concerns that these crucial elements were now at risk. Israel felt relatively comfortable with the leadership of the Egyptian army, viewing it as intimately tied to the US and supportive of the peaceful relationship with Israel. Israel was worried by Islamist and neo-Nasserite elements that played a role in Egypt's new politics and had question marks about the young reformist elements. During the months that followed Mubarak's fall, several incidents revealed the potential for deterioration in the relationship. It transpired that during years of neglect by Mubarak's regime, the central government in Cairo had actually lost control over the Sinai to the Bedouin tribes and that radical, Salafi elements had settled among them. These groups had close connections to Islamist groups in Gaza. Egyptian gas supply to Israel was interrupted several times when terrorists in the Sinai blew up the pipeline. Other terrorist acts were launched directly at Israel. Rockets were fired from the Sinai in the direction of the town of Eilat on the Red Sea. More ominous were terrorist attacks in August 2011 on Israeli buses and vehicles traveling along the Egyptian-Israeli border. In the ensuing fighting, five Egyptian soldiers were killed. The incident was used by radical elements in Cairo to launch an attack on the Israeli Embassy on September 9, 2011. It took direct intervention by President Obama to get the Egyptian military leadership to step in and put an end to a situation that could have had far-reaching consequences.

During the previous thirty years, the Egyptian-Israeli border was so peaceful that Israel refrained from building a security fence along it. It now turned out that this was no longer tenable given the new terrorist threat from the Sinai as well as the large number of African immigrants smuggled by Bedouin networks to the Sinai into Israel where they created an explosive social problem. A fence was indeed built expeditiously.

A new phase began at the end of June 2012 when Mohamed Morsi became Egypt's president. The Muslim Brotherhood had objected all along to the peace with Israel. According to its doctrine, Palestine is Muslim land and Jewish sovereignty over this land cannot be recognized. But once in power, Morsi had to adopt a more pragmatic position. He refrained from tampering with the Egyptian-Israeli peace treaty, refused to deal directly with Israel, and let his military manage the relationship. Morsi and the Muslim Brotherhood were sympathetic to the Hamas government in Gaza, Hamas being the Palestinian branch of the Muslim Brotherhood. But when Hamas's relationship with Israel deteriorated later in 2012 and Israel launched operation "Pillar of Defense" (November 14–21), Morsi refrained from taking any radical action and actually played an important role in negotiating a cease-fire and an end to the military operation.

Israel was a passive observer of the domestic developments in Egypt; the buildup of secular opposition to Morsi and the Muslim Brotherhood's rule, which led on July 3, 2013, to the military takeover, which, behind the façade of a civilian government, placed control in the hands of the minister of defense, General Abdel Fattah el-Sisi. El-Sisi is not particularly friendly to Israel and has continued the policy of keeping the most essential components of the peace treaty and managing the relationship with Israel through discreet military channels. But Israel has in fact welcomed the change in Egypt; it never felt comfortable with Morsi and the Muslim Brotherhood and continued to see the military establishment as its main asset in the Egyptian political arena. Furthermore, as a leader who declared and has conducted an active campaign against the Muslim Brotherhood, el-Sisi also adopted a negative attitude toward the Hamas government in Gaza and has shown the first serious effort in destroying the smuggling industry though the tunnels into Gaza from the northern Sinai. El-Sisi has also tackled the Bedouin and jihadi elements in the Sinai, which he views as threats to Egypt's national security.

Israel realizes that Egypt will probably go through a lengthy period of domestic instability caused by the ongoing conflict between the regime and the Muslim Brotherhood. Having been outlawed, at least part of the organization is likely to go underground and wage terrorist campaigns against the regime. Egypt is likely to be preoccupied with its domestic problems and play a less significant role in the region.

THE SYRIAN CIVIL WAR

For much of the period between March 2011 and the summer of 2013, the Syrian crisis has been the most important regional issue in the Middle East. Within months of the outbreak of the rebellion against Bashar al-Assad's regime, it transpired that this is going to be a long-term conflict, that the regime is unable to quash the rebellion, and that the opposition, while able to take over large parts of the country, is unable to topple the regime. It also transpired that the Syrian crisis has become the arena of regional and international conflicts. Regionally, the conflict between Iran and its rivals has been played out in the Syrian battlefield. Iran has invested on a large scale in protecting the regime by sending military advisers, fighters, supplies, and money. At times it seemed that the regime's campaign is actually managed by the Iranian Revolutionary Guards. Iran has also prevailed on Hezbollah, its

Lebanese proxy, to send thousand of fighters into Syria. At stake for Iran is the preservation of an allied regime that has actually become an Iranian client as well as that of its Lebanese assets. The Iranians realize that a victory in Syria by the Sunni opposition could weaken and possibly destroy Hezbollah's position in Lebanon. On the other side of the dividing line is a loose coalition of the United Sates, its Western European allies, Turkey, Saudi Arabia, Qatar, and Jordan. Each of these states, for its own reasons, would like to see Assad toppled and replaced by one or another part of the Syrian opposition. The "draw" that has characterized the Syrian crisis during most of the period has been altered by a shifting tide in the regime's favor in the spring and early summer of 2013. The regime's victory in Qusayr in June 2013 (much of the fighting was actually done by Hezbollah) was a turning point, reinforced by (ironically) the chemical weapons crisis in August 2013, and the Geneva agreement between Iran and the P5-plus-1.

Israel has chosen as a rule to stay on the sidelines. It has an important stake in the events in Syria and in the outcome of the crisis. Syria is not just a neighboring state but a country with which Israel has intermittently fought and negotiated peace. Syria has kept a quiet cease-fire line with Israel but has waged a campaign against it through Lebanon and Gaza. Syria also presents a military threat due to its arsenal of chemical weapons, ballistic missiles, and other sophisticated weapon systems. Israel has an acute interest in the outcome of the Syrian crisis and in Syria's future. It also recognizes the actual and potential effect that the Syrian crisis has on Syria's neighbors and on the balance of power in the region.

Israeli decision-makers and analysts are roughly divided into two schools with regard to the Syrian crisis. One school, often described as "the devil we know" school, believes Israel's interest would best be served by the survival of Assad's regime. It argues that given the dominant role played within the ranks of the Syrian opposition by jihadi groups affiliated with Al Qaeda, the fall of Assad's regime could lead to the emergence of a "terrorist state" in Syria or to the creation of areas, some of them close to the Israeli border, under the control of the jihadi groups possibly equipped with sophisticated weapon systems taken from the Syrian army. Compared with the threats presented to Israel by such an eventuality, so the argument goes, it is preferable to have Assad stay in power. In any event, it would be a weakened Assad, possibly in control of just part of Syria.

The other school, while recognizing the validity of such threats, argues that Assad's survival would be a victory for a Russian-Iranian-Hezbollah axis with Assad much more submissive to Iran than in earlier years. Members of this school cite the course of the Lebanese War in 2006 to illustrate the threat to Israel should Assad emerge relatively successful from the civil war.

In any event, these are mostly academic arguments. The Israeli government realizes correctly that even if it wanted to, it could not affect the course of the civil war. Any help offered to the opposition would play into the regime's argument that this is not a genuine civil war but a conspiracy hatched from the outside in the service of American and Israeli interests. But Israel defined its own "redlines" in Syria and has announced several times that it will intervene to interdict the transfer of sophisticated weapon systems to Hezbollah or the fall of weapons of mass destruction into terrorist hands. In fact, Israel has acted several times, mostly discreetly, against weapon transfers to Hezbollah. The threat of chemical weapons may well be addressed by the American-Russian agreement accepted by the regime to destroy Syria's arsenal. Israel responded to this agreement with mixed feelings. It welcomed the probable destruction of this arsenal, but it was unhappy with the promotion thus given to Russia's position in the Middle East and by the negative signal sent to Iran by Barack Obama's evident unwillingness to act militarily in Syria. There has been a clear linkage between the Syrian crisis and the issue of Iran's quest for a nuclear weapon. Indeed, Israel has been critical of the interim agreement signed in Geneva, arguing that a much better deal could have been obtained and that the agreement was likely to consolidate Iran's position as a nuclear threshold state.

Even as Assad's regime is doing better in the Syrian civil war, the notion and discussion of

Syria's potential partition has not vanished from the scene. In late 2012 and early 2013, when the regime seemed to be on the verge of defeat, the scenario that was often discussed was that of the Alawites withdrawing to their mountains and creating a "statelet" there, on the coast, in areas east of the mountains with a territorial link to the Shiite parts of Lebanon. It was assumed that in that case the Kurdish minority in northeastern Syria would formalize the status quo into full-fledged autonomy. Such a scenario would have major repercussions for Syria's environment. Syria's politics are closely intertwined with those of Lebanon and Iraq. Hezbollah's role in the fighting in Syria has been mentioned previously, and in Lebanon itself violence spreads as militant Sunni elements and Hezbollah fight an extension of the Syrian civil war. The interplay between Syrian and Iraqi politics is more complex. Nuri Kamal al-Maliki's regime, close to Iran as it is, encourages Shiite volunteers to cross the border into Syria and fight for the regime. The 20 percent Sunni-Arab minority that has lost its traditional ascendency looks to a Sunni victory in Syria as a potential source of support.

The more radical jihadi elements in this minority formed the Islamic State of Iraq and Syria, known as ISIS, a formidable group fighting in the Syrian civil war. The group's name reflects the sense that Iraq's and Syria's fates are intertwined. And while Syria's potential breakup is discussed, it is important to bear in mind that Iraq territory is, in fact, divided into three sectors.

One of these zones is the Kurdish region in Iraq's northern part. But for a formal claim of sovereignty, the Kurdish region enjoys virtual independence. Its leadership knows full well that a quest for formal independence is currently unrealistic primarily due to Turkey's opposition. Turkey has a minority of at least 20 percent Kurds and has traditionally viewed Kurdish aspirations for independence in Iraq as a threat to its own national security. Presently, Turkey and the Iraqi Kurdish leadership have a good relationship predicated on the latter's understanding that sovereignty is not an option. The effect of developments in Syria's Kurdish region on Kurdish-Turkish relations is limited, but Turkey keeps a watchful eye on Syria. Having two autonomous, semi-independent Kurdish regions on its borders would exacerbate the potential danger to Turkey's own stability.

The opening paragraph of this essay mentioned an important motif in Israel's thinking about its position in the region, namely the cultivation of relationships with minority groups against Arab nationalism when the latter seemed to be the major threat to Israel's national security. In that context, Israel extended support to the Kurdish rebels against Iraq's central government in the 1970s and cultivated relations with such groups as the Druze in Syria and the Maronites in Lebanon. The prospect of states in the region breaking up and minority groups playing a more important role could, in theory, raise fresh Israeli thoughts about partnering with such groups. So far, Israel has avoided such temptations. Its view of the "great unraveling" is ambivalent. It realizes that direct threats to its national security have been weakened, but it also understands that anarchy and disorder could breed other threats. And as Israel is negotiating with the Palestinian Authority, maintains peaceful relationships with Egypt and Jordan, as well as discreet relations with Arab states in the

Gulf and North Africa, the "zero-sum-game" outlook of the 1940s and 1950s is less relevant.

REPERCUSSIONS FOR LEBANON

In the 1950s and 1960s the conventional wisdom in Israel was that "Lebanon will be the second Arab state to make peace with Israel." Underlying this cliché was the assumption that as a state dominated by Christian Maronite elements, Lebanon implicitly saw itself as allied with Israel, another non-Arab Muslim state in the Middle East confronting similar challenges by Muslim and Arab nationalist forces. Indeed, negotiations were conducted and some understandings were reached between the leadership of prestate Israel and religious and secular leaders of the Maronite community. Israeli policymakers and analysts believed that Lebanon's leadership would be happy to establish a formal peaceful relationship with Israel, but they also saw that a state led by a minority group did not have the power and legitimacy required to be the first to break the Arab taboo and would therefore be able to do so only in the wake of a more powerful mainstream Arab state like Egypt, Syria, or Iraq.

With the passage of years, Lebanon was transformed by demographic and political changes and the Lebanese-Israeli border became another active arena of Arab-Israel hostilities. In the late 1970s and early 1980s, an alliance was created between Israel, led at the time by Menachem Begin and Ariel Sharon, and a segment of the Maronite community and the Phalange Party led by Bashir Gemayel. This alliance culminated in the Israeli invasion of Lebanon in 1982 and Gemayel's election, with Israel's help, as Lebanon's president. This ill-conceived adventure ended in a disaster affecting all those involved and left a "Lebanese trauma" in Israel. Less than three weeks after his election, Gemayel was killed by a massive bomb in the headquarters of his party. His older brother Amin was chosen as his successor. But he was a different kind of political man, and he was to take Lebanon into the orbit of Syria. Israel and Lebanon signed a peace treaty of sorts in 1983, but it was not a legitimate, durable agreement and had no real value.

Lebanon, thus, was not the second Arab state to sign a peace treaty with Israel, nor is it likely to be the third. Israel retained a security zone in south Lebanon that became a battlefield between itself and Hezbollah, the party cum militia cum terrorist organization built in Lebanon by the Ayatollah's regime in Tehran. Iran and Syria shared turf in Lebanon while preserving the formal structure of a Lebanese state headed by a Maronite Christian.

Israel withdrew from Lebanon in 2000 to the international boundary and watched nervously as Iran built an arsenal of more than 20,000 rockets and missiles held by Hezbollah as a deterrent against an Israeli attack on either Iran or Syria. Despite the trauma of 1982 and the subsequent years, Israel under Prime Minister Ehud Olmert, provoked by Hezbollah, launched a second Lebanese war in 2006 which ended with mixed results. It was the classic case of the "asymmetrical wars" that Israel now has to wage in the "new Middle East." Israel's failure to achieve a clear-cut victory was widely perceived as a Hezbollah victory as well as an achievement for its two patrons, Iran and Syria. But the damage inflicted

ITAMAR RABINOVICH

on Lebanon has served as an effective deterrent against Hezbollah's attacks. Hezbollah's arsenal of rockets and missiles has been replenished by Iran and is now estimated to contain about 50,000 pieces. The Lebanese-Israeli front thus remains a tinderbox that could be ignited at any time. Hezbollah's larger arsenal includes long-range rockets that can be fired from central and northern Lebanon and inflict serious damage across Israel. The estimate is that if this happens, Israel would have to occupy much of Lebanon as well as inflict massive damage on the country's infrastructure.

Israel watches closely as Hezbollah is fighting on Assad's behalf in Syria, the Syrian crisis spills into Lebanon itself when radical Sunni elements plant bombs in Hezbollah strongholds in Beirut, Alawites and Sunnis are fighting in Tripoli, and Sunni politicians are assassinated by Hezbollah or other Syrian proxies. Hezbollah has been weakened by its role in the Syrian crisis. There is criticism within the Shiite community and elsewhere in Lebanon over Lebanese men dying in Syria, for the preservation of Assad's regime in the service of Iran. Hezbollah has also suffered serious casualties in the fighting, a loss balanced to some extent by experience gained by its troops. What is glaringly missing in Lebanon is an alternative political force that could take advantage of these circumstances and reassert the Lebanese state's sovereignty. In March 2005, a camp opposing Iran, Syria, and Hezbollah was able to flood the streets of Beirut and force a Syrian military withdrawal. That camp has since disintegrated. It would probably take a victory by the Syrian opposition for these circumstances to change and for Lebanese politics to undertake a different course. Israel is a passive witness of these developments. The dominant view in the country in the aftermath of two unsuccessful wars and a massive failed investment is that Israel should avoid a direct involvement in Lebanese politics and should count on its ability to deter rather than intervene.

RAMIFICATIONS FOR THE PALESTINIAN ARENA

The outbreak of the Arab Spring raised, from Israel's perspective, two main questions in the

Palestinian context: Will there be a "Palestinian Spring" in the form of popular pressure on either the Palestinian Authority or the Hamas government in Gaza to reform and democratize? And, will the effect of popular uprisings in the Arab world propel the Palestinians to launch a third intifada?

There were manifestations of effervescence in the West Bank and the Gaza Strip against the authoritarian rules (milder in the West Bank) in both elements of the Palestinian Authority. In the West Bank, Mahmoud Abbas skillfully handled the popular pressure by taking the Palestinian issue to the United Nations. He was not successful in obtaining a General Assembly or Security Council vote that would recognize full Palestinian independence and sovereignty, but he did improve the legal and international standing of the Palestinian Authority, bringing it closer to being a state. His rhetoric in Arabic directed at his constituency clearly reflected his view and argument that this was the Palestinian version of an Arab Spring.

The Hamas leadership in Gaza was far more deeply affected by the broader changes in the

region. For one thing, it lost its important connections with Iran and Syria primarily due to
the civil war in Syria. As a Sunni movement, the
Palestinian branch of the Muslim Brotherhood,
Hamas could not remain a close ally and client
of Shiite Iran and Assad's regime as the latter
two were waging a brutal war against Syria's
Sunnis. Hamas had to close its external headquarters in Damascus and lost most, if not all,
the support it had been receiving from Iran. As
long as Mohamed Morsi and the Muslim Brotherhood were in power in Egypt, Hamas could
feel that this was more than adequate compensation for the loss of its original patrons. Egypt,
after all, was a neighboring state, its support
much more direct and immediate, and its new
friends in Cairo facilitated Hamas's access to
and from the Gaza Strip. But with the change in
Egypt and the emergence of a semi-military
regime hostile to the Muslim Brotherhood and
determined to restore Egyptian control of the
Sinai, Hamas's position took a radical turn for
the worse.

These events were unfolding as Israel was governed by Netanyahu's right-wing coalitions. The

Israel-Palestinian negotiation made no progress, the settlement project in the West Bank was reinforced, and the settlers were emboldened. This began to change in late 2013 as the Obama administration, led by Secretary of State John Kerry, revived the quest for an Israeli-Palestinian settlement with fresh determination and enthusiasm. The prospects of Kerry's ambitious efforts to resolve, or at least move forward, the Israeli-Palestinian peace process have yet to be fully tested, but the diplomatic effort has been accompanied by a rise in tension and violence in the West Bank.

In Israel, the debate over the Palestinian issue between Right and Left has been exacerbated by these developments. The debate is first and foremost about Israel's identity and future, about security and demography. But it also has to do with Israel's position in the region and relationship with the larger Arab world. The proponents of a diplomatic solution, painful as it may be, argue among other things that a resolution of the Israeli-Palestinian conflict, or at least a significant movement in this direction, is key to a different relationship with Israel's neighbors and an opportunity to take part in shaping the region through diplomacy rather than force.

TURKEY'S REGIONAL ROLE

Israel's relationship with Turkey has seen a number of ups and downs since 1948. Turkey welcomed Israel's establishment, and it was significant for the young Jewish state to be recognized by and have diplomatic relations with a major Muslim country. In the late 1950s Turkey, together with Iran and Ethiopia, was Israel's partner in an unannounced pro-Western regional coalition. In subsequent decades, Israel's allies in Turkey were members of the Kemalist establishment, first and foremost the Turkish military, while Islamist and leftist groups tried to downgrade the relationship when they had power or influence. In the 1990s, a close strategic alliance between Israel and Turkey thrived. This changed during the first decade of the current century. In 2003, Recep Tayyip Erdogan and the AKP, an Islamist party, came to power and gradually distanced themselves from Israel. This was motivated by their Islamist worldview, support for the Palestinian cause in general and Hamas in particular, and the quest for a leadership role in the Middle East and the Arab world. Having been rebuffed by the European Union, Turkey was looking to build its influence and hegemonic position in its immediate environment. Distance from Israel was replaced by open hostility, particularly after the Mavi Marmara incident in 2010, when the Israeli navy took over a Turkish ship, dispatched probably with unofficial permission to break the siege of Gaza.

Relations have since improved. The dispute over the Mavi Marmara incident is practically resolved, and while the alliance of the 1990s is not likely to be restored as long as Erdogan is in power, the overall relationship is improving. This development has much to do with the failure of Turkey's effort to build a hegemonic position in the Arab world. Its support for the Muslim Brotherhood in Egypt has led to tension with General el-Sisi and his regime and, still more important, Erdogan's initial success in turning Bashar al-Assad into a junior partner in a new relationship was replaced by a problematic involvement in the Syrian civil war. Erdogan has supported the Syrian opposition both as a Sunni Islamist leader and a disappointed patron resenting Assad's failure to heed his advice and respond politically to the opposition's demands and offer reform and participation. Erdogan, after all, was casting himself and Turkey as a model of Islamist democracy. As a neighboring state, Turkey offered the opposition hospitality for its political headquarters, has facilitated the transfer of weapons and funds to the opposition, and has taken in a large number of Syrian refugees. But in time, Erdogan's Syrian policy met with increasing difficulties. First and foremost, it exposed the structural weaknesses of the Turkish state. The Alawite population in the former Syrian province of Hatay, and the large Shiite minority known as Alevis (not Alawite, but supportive of them), are critical of the government's Syrian policy. The prospect of Syria's breakdown as a state and an emergence of a second Kurdish autonomous region on Turkey's borders is alarming to Ankara. The domestic problems faced by Erdogan's government that are unrelated to these events further weakened his capacity to wage an effective regional policy.

These trends are viewed by Israel as offering a new opportunity. Mending relations with Turkey, let alone building a new, closer collaboration with this Middle Eastern power, would be an important asset for Israel's policy in the region. This explains Israel's willingness to overcome domestic right-wing pressure, apologize for the Mavi Marmara incident, and offer compensation to the families of the Turkish victims of the violence on board that ship.

A NEW REGIONAL ORDER

As has been mentioned above, the regional politics of the Middle East during the past three decades have been deeply affected by the return of Iran and Turkey as full-fledged players in this arena. The changes in US policy in the region under Barack Obama and Russia's quest to restore at least some of the former Soviet Union's assets in the region have had a similar effect on the regional scene.

Mention has been made of the ebb and flow of Erdogan's policy in the Middle East. What seemed in the middle of this century's first decade to be a successful bid for regional hegemony ended in failure. At that time, Turkey was or portrayed itself as a military-economic power, a successful model of Islamic democracy, a source of inspiration for Middle Eastern countries looking for economic recovery and a system of governance reconciling their Islamic and Arab identities with a more democratic political system. Erdogan also portrayed himself as a champion of the Palestinian cause, specifically of Hamas in Gaza. As we have seen, this drive has recently been deflated by a series of failures in the region and by the cracks revealed in Turkey's political infrastructure and Erdogan's government. But Turkey remains an important and relatively powerful actor clearly in search of a redefinition of its role.

Iran's quest for regional hegemony has an older history. The Islamic Revolution of 1979 was seeking, as revolutions do, to export itself. For many years its only success was in Lebanon, where it built a powerful base through its proxy, Hezbollah. It also built a close and effective alliance with the Baath regime of Hafez al-Assad.

Its efforts to influence the Shiite populations in the Gulf were less successful. Throughout this period Iran was building a powerful military and engaged in a program designed to acquire a nuclear arsenal. In the aftermath of 2003, Iran's efforts have accelerated, more ambitious goals have been set, and more impressive successes scored. The toppling of Saddam Hussein's regime and America's failed intervention in Iraq removed an important barrier to the projection of Iranian influence westward. In Syria, Hafez al-Assad's successor, Bashar, a much weaker person and ruler, was converted from a partner to a client. In Lebanon, Hezbollah overcame the adversity of 2005 and took advantage of its relative success in the 2006 war to reinforce its position as the dominant force in the country. With its influence in Syria, position in Lebanon, and investment in the Hamas government in Gaza, Iran managed to plant itself on three of Israel's borders. It also revealed its far-reaching imperial ambitions by sending a warship through the Suez Canal (allowed by Mubarak's successors after January 2011) to the Mediterranean. The initial events of the Arab Spring, particularly the outbreak of resistance and violence in Bahrain and Yemen, were seen as Iranian successes and a threat to its principal adversary in the Gulf, Saudi Arabia.

But Iran's major effort during this period was to continue its drive for a nuclear arsenal, to enrich uranium, to engage in a parallel construction of a plutonium option, and to develop the wherewithal required for weaponizing and acquiring medium- and long-range missiles capable of carrying nuclear warheads. This effort was carried out while Iran was gaining time through sophisticated negotiations with the international community, conducted under the shadow of an Israeli threat to attack Iran's nuclear installations and vague American statements that "all options are on the table." It is understood by all actors in the region that a nuclear arsenal in Iran would alter the regional balance.

Since January 2009, the Obama administration has conducted a Middle East policy predicated on the assumption that statecraft could be implemented effectively without force. Barack Obama's principal aims in the Middle East were stated clearly during his campaign and in the early weeks of his presidency: to end America's conflict and tension with the Muslim and Arab worlds, to encourage political reform and democratization in the Arab world, to "engage" with both Iran and Syria, and to bring about an end to the Israeli-Palestinian conflict. Obama stated repeatedly that he will not allow Iran to acquire a nuclear weapon and implied that he was willing to use military force to that end or tolerate an Israeli raid on Iran. Having sustained several setbacks during the first two years of his administration, the US president temporarily abandoned some of his policy goals in the Middle East in the latter part of that term, but he came back to his original track after his reelection.

Obama's policy with regard to the principal issue in the Middle East at that time, the Syrian crisis, has been governed by his lessons from Iraq and Afghanistan, namely a determination not to be drawn into military involvement in a third Middle Eastern conflict. This policy was severely tested in the summer of 2013, when Bashar al-Assad's regime used chemical weapons on a massive scale against its own population, thus crossing the "red line" defined by

Obama in August 2012. The US president was clearly reluctant to punish Assad and was released from his dilemma by Vladimir Putin's offer to negotiate the liquidation of Syria's chemical weapons arsenal. This was an achievement of sorts for American diplomacy, but it came with a triple price tag: a boost to Russia's position in the Middle East, an indication to Iran that the US president was not likely to use a military option against its nuclear program, and a lease on life for the Syrian president. This was followed by the interim agreement reached in Geneva in November 2013 between Iran and the P5-plus-1 with regard to its nuclear program. This agreement was preceded by secret US-Iranian negotiations.

The effectiveness of this agreement has yet to be tested. Iran and its interlocutors have yet to agree on its implementation and have yet to negotiate the transition from an interim to a permanent agreement. But in the Sunni parts of the Arab world it is widely suspected that the American-Iranian negotiations that preceded the November accord have actually led to a much broader understanding, that the US may well recognize

Iran's regional role. Such suspicions were reinforced in January 2014 when Secretary Kerry followed his British and French colleagues in saying that Iran could play a role in the Geneva II meeting scheduled for later that month—with all the uncertainties that surround such a meeting. Needless to say, US recognition of Iran's quest for a leading role in the region's politics would transform the current regional order. Some Arab states, Saudi Arabia in particular, have reacted to the prospect with dismay and anger. Saudi Arabia's decision not to join the Security Council as well as several angry statements by Saudi policy-makers reflect Riyadh's anger at Obama and his policies. This mood is also affected by a longer-range Saudi concern that as the US becomes less dependent on Middle Eastern oil, more radical changes in its conduct in the region can be expected. Other Gulf states, reacting differently than the larger, more powerful Saudi Arabia, are hedging their bets by building their own channels to Iran.

The change in Saudi Arabia's mood is reflected not just in expressions of anger at Washington but also in the adoption of a far more assertive regional policy different from the discreet, indirect style of Saudi foreign and regional policy in the past. The Saudis intervened forcefully in Bahrain, actively opposed Morsi while supporting el-Sisi in Egypt, and announced a $3 billion gift to the Lebanese army in order to shore it up as a counter force to Hezbollah. It also continues to play a leading role in support of the Syrian opposition; the formation of *al-Jabha al-Islamiyyah* (the Islamic Front), an umbrella organization for Islamist organizations that are opposed to both Assad's regime and the jihadi groups in Syria, is one important indication of this Saudi activity.

Israel is thus facing a new and changing regional order: a lingering crisis in countries like Syria, Iraq, and Lebanon; a receding American role; the prospect of American compliance with Iran's regional role; a more prominent role played by Putin's Russia; an Egypt preoccupied primarily with its domestic issues; an active and assertive Saudi Arabia; and a reconsideration of Turkish regional policy by Erdogan's government. Some of these developments pose threats to Israel's national security and diplomatic position, but

Israel could also take advantage of some of these changes in order to become a more active and legitimate player in the region's politics. For this to happen, Israel should take advantage of the massive effort invested by Secretary Kerry in order to bring about an Israeli-Palestinian final status agreement. A final status agreement as such may not be feasible at present, but significant progress could be achieved and Israel can improve its regional and international position by offering the right response to Kerry's initiative. Israel can also continue to improve its relationship with Turkey. A return to the intimate alliance of the 1990s is not in the cards, but a reasonably good relationship and a measure of cooperation in issues of common interest such as the Syrian crisis are definitely possible. The change in Saudi Arabia's policy produced much talk of Israeli-Saudi cooperation. This is premature but tacit; indirect coordination is now possible.

SOURCE NOTES

For more on Shimon Peres's concept of the Arab-Israeli peace, see Shimon Peres and Arye Naor, *The New Middle East* (New York: Henry Holt & Co., 1993).

Fouad Ajami describes and nimbly analyzes Hosni Mubarak's regime and its policy regarding anti-Semitism and anti-Israeli propaganda in "The Orphaned Peace," *The Dream Palace of the Arabs: A Generation's Odyssey* (New York: Vintage Books, 1998).

For a fuller version of Benjamin Netanyahu's words on Middle East peace, see *A Place among the Nations: Israel and the World* (Bantam, 1993).

Natan Sharansky's and Ron Dermer's *The Case for Democracy: The Power of Freedom to Overcome Tyranny & Terror* (Public Affairs, 2004) elaborates on the need for democratic transition in the Arab world.

For more on Natan Sharansky's response to the Arab Spring, see "The West Should Bet on Freedom in Egypt," *Washington Post,* December 17, 2011.

A very useful analysis of the Israeli discourse on the Arab Spring is an essay by Lior Lehrs, included in Nimrod Goren and Jenya Yudkevitch, "Israel and the Arab Spring: Opportunities through the Change" (Mitvim, 2013), 7–20.

To read more on Benjamin Netanyahu's speeches during the Arab Spring, please see Lior Lehrs's essay, "Israel and the Arab Spring: Opportunities through the Change."

For additional reading on the Obama administration and its Middle East policies, see Robert M. Gates, *Duty: Memoirs of a Secretary at War* (Knopf, 2014).

ABOUT THE AUTHOR

ITAMAR RABINOVICH, president of the Israel Institute, served as Israel's ambassador to Washington and chief negotiator with Syria and was president of Tel Aviv University. He is professor emeritus of Middle Eastern history at Tel Aviv University, Distinguished Global Professor at New York University (NYU), and the Bronfman Distinguished Nonresident Fellow at the Saban Center for Middle East Policy at the Brookings Institution. His most recent book is *The Lingering Conflict: Israel, the Arabs, and the Middle East, 1948–2011* (Brookings Institution Press, 2012).

HERBERT AND JANE DWIGHT
WORKING GROUP ON
ISLAMISM AND THE
INTERNATIONAL ORDER

The Herbert and Jane Dwight Working Group on Islamism and the International Order seeks to engage in the task of reversing Islamic radicalism through reforming and strengthening the legitimate role of the state across the entire Muslim world. Efforts will draw on the intellectual resources of an array of scholars and practitioners from within the United States and abroad, to foster the pursuit of modernity, human flourishing, and the rule of law and reason in Islamic lands—developments that are critical to the very order of the international system.

The Working Group is cochaired by Hoover fellows Fouad Ajami and Charles Hill, with an active participation by Hoover Institution Director John Raisian. Current core membership includes Russell A. Berman and Abbas Milani, with contributions from Zeyno Baran, Marius Deeb, Reuel Marc Gerecht, Ziad Haider, R. John Hughes, Nibras Kazimi, Bernard Lewis, Habib C. Malik, Camille Pecastaing, Itamar Rabinovich, Lieutenant Colonel Joel Rayburn, Lee Smith, Samuel Tadros, Joshua Teitelbaum, and Tunku Varadarajan.

Freedom or Terror: Europe Faces Jihad
Russell A. Berman

The Myth of the Great Satan:
A New Look at America's Relations with Iran
Abbas Milani

Torn Country: Turkey between Secularism and Islamism
Zeyno Baran

Islamic Extremism and the War of Ideas: Lessons from Indonesia
R. John Hughes

The End of Modern History in the Middle East
Bernard Lewis

The Wave: Man, God, and the Ballot Box in the Middle East
Reuel Marc Gerecht

Trial of a Thousand Years: World Order and Islamism
Charles Hill

Jihad in the Arabian Sea
Camille Pecastaing

The Syrian Rebellion
Fouad Ajami

Motherland Lost: The Egyptian and Coptic Quest for Modernity
Samuel Tadros

Iraq after America: Strongmen, Sectarians, Resistance
Joel Rayburn

[For a list of essays published under the auspices of the
WORKING GROUP ON ISLAMISM AND THE INTERNATIONAL ORDER,
please see page ii.]

INDEX